I0161761

HOW ARE YOU FEELING TODAY?

MONOLOGUES FOR CHILDREN

By
Sabat Beatto

How are you feeling today?
Sabat Beatto

Copyright 2019 Sabat Beatto

All rights reserved. No part of this book may be reproduced in any form without permission in writing from the writer, except by a reviewer.

ISBN: 978-1-7337532-2-7
Manufactured in the United States of America

TABLE OF CONTENTS

DEDICATION

Ms. Lanfranco

Ms. Soberanis

Ms. Alam

Class 2/3-317

Special thanks to Mr. Mazun for his advice and input throughout the writing of this book.

INTRODUCTION

Among all the human age groups, children are the most emotionally sensitive. This is something we don't even realize in our daily lives. A person need not have a degree in psychology to understand what is happening in a child's life. By having a little curiosity and concern, you can easily figure out if a child is living a stable life or he/she is going through social issues like financial deficiencies, parental issues, bullying, etc. These factors affect a child's mental health negatively and these negative effects are reflected in that child's academic performance. In schools, teachers are dealing with over 20 students simultaneously. This is the reason they cannot care or bother about what a child is going through in his/her personal life and what he wants from his/her teachers or from people in his/her life in general. A child who has not eaten properly or sees a fight in his house every day cannot perform as well as a child living a stable and joyous life. This is why Sabat Beatto's book "how are you feeling today?" is so significant for understanding an average child's psychology. In this brief book, the author has directly connected with the students, asking them a very simple question, and through that method, he can figure out what a child is going through in his social and personal life. This method can be very useful for teachers and parents who desire to interact properly with their students or children. This book may also introduce a new theory, The Mood Meter, created by Marc Brackett. Marc A. Brackett is the Founding Director of the Yale Center for Emotional Intelligence and Professor in the Child Study Center at Yale University. According to the author, "The Mood Meter is designed to help us learn to recognize emotions, in ourselves and others, with increasing subtlety and to develop strategies for regulating (or managing) those emotions. It provides us with a "language" to talk about our feelings."

"How are you feeling today?" is a brief book based on monologues that reflect children's feelings and psychiatric traits. This book includes a model that is extremely effective in understanding a child's psychiatric condition. This model would help teachers to improve their student's social life and also improve their academic records. Asking a student about how he feels at the beginning of every lecture is something undoable. All you need is to take care of your students and treat them with love, care, and concern.

HOW ARE FEELING TODAY?

WHAT COLOR ARE YOU AT TODAY?

MY MOM AND DAD BOUGHT ME A DOG

'm in the color orange. I'm feeling so happy! My mom and dad bought me a dog, and I named him Rocky. He is beige and brown. He likes to play a lot, so I take him out and, together, we play. I'm teaching him how to sit and do some other tricks. I throw him a ball, and he brings it back, sometimes. He likes to eat. We got him a red bowl and a red collar. I like to walk him outside. He makes me smile.

Rocky loves belly rubs. He lays on his back a lot to be patted on his belly. Sometimes he licks my hand. Mom and Dad laugh when we play. Rocky follows me when I run, and I chase after him when he runs. He is my best friend. Mom said Rocky lived at a shelter, but now he has a warm bed. It makes me feel happy when I think about him.

That's wonderful to hear! Dogs can be wonderful friends and great companions. Even though dogs can be a great responsibility, it sounds like you are taking very good care of him.

TRUMP WANTS TO SEND MY DAD BACK TO MEXICO

'm feeling sad because my dad must hide at home. Trump wants to send him back to Mexico, so my dad can't work anymore. The place where he was working doesn't want my dad because he's an illegal immigrant. I'm sad because I don't want my dad to leave. That will disrupt my education and the friendships I have created. My dad loves his job, and I know he wants to go to work. I wish he could go back there.

At home, my dad waits. He always worries about bills and other expenses while my mom works. My mom worries about money and bills, too, so sometimes she must work double shifts. This is killing her, of course, but she has to do what she has to do to make sure the family is taken care of. I hope that my dad's papers come soon. He wishes to relieve my mom of this stress quickly. We don't know when that will happen. I feel sad when I remember my dad hiding from the police.

I'm sorry to hear that. I know it must be very hard on you to know that your parents are going through this, but it sounds like your dad's papers are on the way. Just know that whatever happens, your mom and dad will do their best for you.

MY LITTLE SISTER DID NOT LET ME SLEEP LAST NIGHT

feel tired. I'm exhausted today because I couldn't sleep last night. My little sister was crying all night. Mom gave her medicine for her teeth, but she still cried... and cried. When I was about to sleep, it was time to wake up to come to school. I wish I could be in bed right now. Teacher, I want to sleep. I wish I could rest instead of writing or doing the math assignment you assigned.

Teething can be so disturbing. When Mom gives her a bottle, she stops. I wish her teeth would stop hurting. Then maybe she'll sleep and not cry. I wish I could sleep now. When it's time to go home from school, I'm going right to my bed. Then I can rest and not feel so tired. I hope I don't have a lot of homework to do.

Tell you what – just for today, I will not give you any homework to do so that when it's time to go home, you can go right to bed. Your sister's teething will not last long, but in the meantime, ask your mother for some earplugs so you can sleep better.

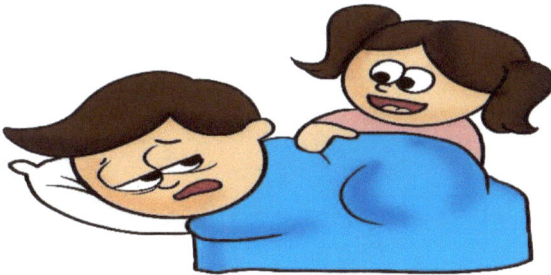

MOM CAN'T PAY THE RENT

Teacher, I'm worried. My mom can't pay the rent. She said she has to have a second job because she doesn't make enough money to pay the rent. The owner of the house told my mom she had to move out if she doesn't pay the rent. My mom cried, and I'm so worried. I want to help my mom, but I can't work. I'm only 8 years old. If Mom doesn't get a job soon, we will have to live on the streets. I don't want to leave our house.

My stomach feels nervous. I want to help my mom. I don't like it when she's sad. I want to see her smile instead. My mom is a good worker. She must get a second job, and then she can pay the rent. We want to stay in our house. I wish I knew what would happen. It makes me feel worried to think about it, but I can't help it. I hope my mom can pay the rent soon.

Try not to worry. Your mother is very smart and will do her best to help you stay in the house. Perhaps you can make her happy by asking what you can do to help.

MY DAD IS MOVING OUT

I feel sad. My dad and mom were fighting the other night. My dad told my mom that he's moving out of the apartment. They argue a lot, especially during the night. I don't know who I will live with. My mom said I'll stay with her, but we must move to a smaller apartment. I won't have a personal room. I'll sleep with my mom on the same bed. My dad told me I should move out with him, so I'll have a room to myself. I don't know what to do. I wish I could go to the moon, Saturn, or somewhere farther away.

I want my dad to stay and not move out. I wish my mom and dad could stop fighting. If they stopped fighting, my father wouldn't have to move out. He could stay. But how will I choose who to live with if he doesn't? I mean, I love them both. I'll miss my friends at the apartment when we move away. I can see them at school, but we won't be able to play together anymore. Teacher, I'm unfortunate.

I'm so sorry to hear that. Just know that whatever happens, your parents love you and they will do their best to take care of you. I know this is hard but maybe you can stay with both parts of the time.

MY GRANDMA DIED

Teacher, I feel sad. My grandma just died, and I don't know how to get over it. Everybody loved my grandma, and I liked her, too. On weekends, when we visited her, she made arepas. She used to comb my hair every night. I really do miss my Abuelita. I went to cook with her one more time before she passed away. Who will cook with me now? Her company seems irreplaceable.

My grandma had a big laugh. When she laughed, it made everyone laugh. She liked to tease my mother. She would laugh with my parents a lot. She had big silver and blue rings. I could play with them if I promised not to lose them. I never lost one, ever. I wish I could see my Abuelita again. I'll love her forever.

I'm so sorry your Abuelita died. It will be hard, at first, and I know you will miss her, but just know that if you keep happy memories of her with you, you will feel better.

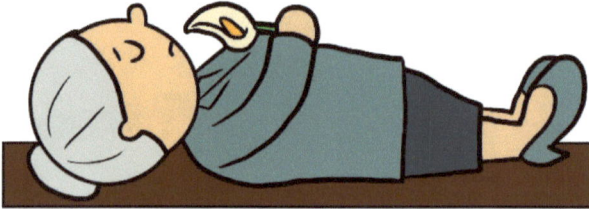

MY PARENTS BOUGHT A NEW HOME

I am so excited! My parents bought a new home. We're moving in next week. It's a huge house. I will have a whole room for myself. My dad said we will decorate it all in pink. I'm so eager. I can have a pink bed, and I don't have to share a room with my brother anymore. He will have his own room, and he will pick a color for it, too. I guess he'll choose green for his room.

It is hard to wait to move! I wish we could move in today. We will have a big yard to run in, and I will ride my bike on the street. Dad says the street is safe and long. Now I have an Olympic track; I'll race my brother! I'm so happy!

That's fantastic, having your own room will be wonderful! Just be careful when you race your brother on the street. Wear your bike helmet and remember to watch out for cars, okay?

SOMEONE IS BULLYING ME

'm feeling sad. Someone is bullying me. He calls me 'fat,' 'chubby,' and 'pig.' It makes me so sad when he does that. I try and stay away from him, but it doesn't work. He delights in taunting me. Even if I eat a carrot, he calls me fat. I don't like to eat lunch at school anymore. It is affecting me.

The teacher told him to stop, but he would not. Now he waits for the teacher to go away. I want him to go away, too. Sometimes I laugh, but I never think it's funny. I don't know why he doesn't like me. I'm always nice to him. It's not fair. I feel sad because I don't know what to do to make him stop. I don't like bullying.

The best thing to do is to ignore him. There is no reason he should be bullying you. If you ignore him and it doesn't help, please let me know, and I will do my best to make it stop.

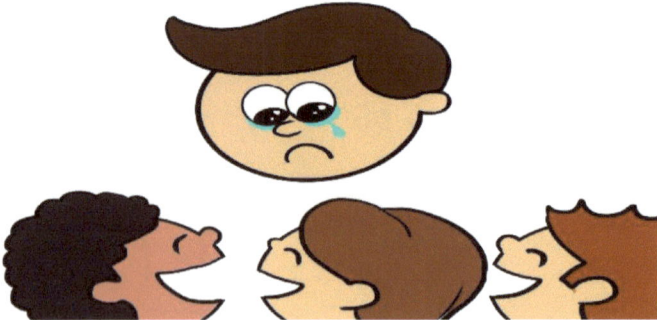

I'M LOSING MY HEARING

I'm afraid. Yesterday the doctor told me that I'm going to lose my hearing. My mom brought me to get my ears checked. Sometimes I can't hear my mom. Sometimes I can't hear my teacher or my friends. So, we went to the doctor to check my ears. I don't understand why I will lose my hearing. How will I cope? It is hard to think about.

The doctor said I must see another doctor, too. My mom said maybe something could help my ears. I don't like going to see the doctor. I'm afraid it will hurt to check my ears. If I lose my hearing, it will be hard to be in school. I'm worried about not hearing. When I'm afraid, I like to be with my mom.

Please, try not to be afraid. The doctors are there to help you and not hurt you in any way. I know it's scary, but just know that your doctors and your mom are there to take care of you.

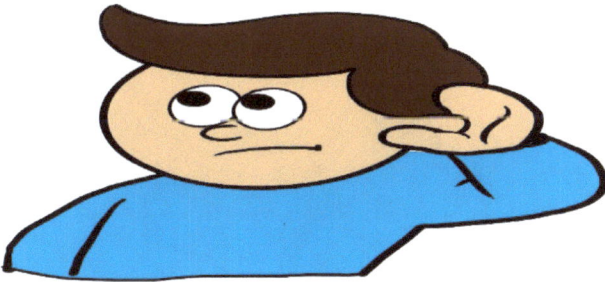

I CAN'T BRING IN SCHOOL SUPPLIES

Mr. B, I'm so sad. My mom doesn't have money to buy school supplies. My mom is the only one who's working. She must pay rent, buy food, and clothing. I came to school without my supplies. My teacher asked me where my supplies were, and I was too shy to answer. All my friends brought supplies but not me. I felt like the ground should open and swallow me.

The teacher smiled and said, "Not to worry." But I still feel sad. I wish my mom could have more money. But she already works all the time. I don't want anyone to know that I didn't bring supplies.

Don't worry; I'll tell nobody. You can be late on the course of the year. Your teacher will understand.

MY MOM IS HAVING A BABY

I feel excited! My mom is having a baby! I see she has a big stomach now. I don't know if it will be a girl or a boy. We'll find out when the new baby comes. I hope it's a girl so I can have a sister to play with. I promise I'll share my toys with her. My mom says the baby will sleep in a crib in her and my dad's room. But I hope she sleeps in my room, too. I will stay quiet so she can rest.

My best friend has a new brother. He cries a lot, but my new baby won't cry as much because I'll help take care of it! My mom says her stomach will get even bigger! Pretty soon, I won't fit on her lap. I wonder if the baby will have long fingers like me. I'm so excited for the new baby! I can't wait to have it.

You will have a wonderful time with your new baby brother or sister. No matter if it's a boy or girl, I know you will love them and have lots of fun playing and helping to take care of them.

I'M GOING TO PLAY SOCCER

'm feeling happy. My mom said I could play soccer, so I'm going to practice after school. I play soccer at home with my friends all the time, but this will be on a team! I like to run and score goals. I'm very good at soccer. We'll have games on the weekends, and my dad can come to watch me on the sets.

My mom has to buy me some cleats and shin guards. I can only wear them when I play soccer. I can't wear my cleats in the house because my mom says the floor will get scratched. I wish to step up my practice. Only four more days until soccer starts! Our first game is on Saturday. I can't wait to play.

I'm so proud of you! You will have a great time playing soccer, and your mom is right; try not to wear your cleats in the house.

I'M THE TALLEST IN MY CLASS

'm feeling shy. We took our class picture, and I had to stand in the back. I had to stand in the back because I'm the tallest kid. I'm taller than all the boys. One boy makes fun of me and calls me 'giraffe.' I am surprised some kids would call name for almost anything. I don't like it when he does that. I wish I had the same height as the other kids.

My dad said that the other kids would grow too. I was just the first to develop. I want them to grow soon so I won't be the tallest. I think if they ate healthy food like me, they would be taller. I don't like it when the other kids look at me. I just want to be quiet and not talk to them. I don't want to take another class picture. It's hard to be the tallest kid.

Being tall has its advantages, and if other kids are making fun of you, it's because they are envious. Your father is right.

MY PAINTING IS IN THE ART SHOW

I'm feeling proud. My class is having an art show. My painting was chosen to be hung up. Everyone will see my artwork. I hope they like it. I painted a big green field. Horses are running in the field. Birds are flying in the sky. The birds were hard to paint because they're so small. I painted a blue pond in the middle of the field for the horses to drink. My painting has a lot of colors. My teacher said she liked all the colors I used.

I'm happy that my mom and dad will see my painting hanging up in my class. My dad loves horses, and I know he'll like my creation. My mom does a lot of art projects with me. She'll be proud to see my painting in the art show.

You are right to be proud; it sounds like painting is something you love to do. Keep at it.

I'M LEFT OUT

I'm feeling left out. My sister always plays with the boy across the street and I don't. Sometimes I play too, but usually, they say, "No." I want to play with them. One day, I was also playing, and then my sister told me to go home. I told my mom, and my sister got in trouble. My mom said I should be included.

There are lots of games for three kids. We can play tag, we can play hide and seek, and we can ride our bikes, but sometimes they say no. They don't want to play those games, so I play by myself. Playing alone is boring. It makes me feel lonely when I see them playing together. I wish I could play, too.

I know it's frustrating. If your sister does not want to play with you and the boy together, then there are other kids you can play with.

I'M HUNGRY AT BEDTIME

I feel hungry. Last night we didn't have dinner. My mom made some toast and that was all we had to eat. Our fridge was empty, and mom said she couldn't go for food shopping until Friday. Since we don't have enough money for food, we eat at my aunt's house for dinner sometimes. Last time, she made us macaroni and cheese. It was good. I wish we had dinner over there last night.

It's hard to sleep when my stomach is rumbling as a result of hunger. I feel grumpy when there's nothing to eat. When I come to school, I want three breakfasts! I always eat all my lunch. My brother had some chips, but he didn't give me any. I do share with him. I hope tonight we can go to my aunt's house for dinner. I can't imagine going to bed without food.

I'm sorry to hear that. It's good that your aunt is there for you to help your mom. It sounds like she cares for you a lot.

I DIDN'T GO TO THE SLEEPOVER

'm embarrassed. My best friend had a sleepover party, but I didn't go. Sometimes at night, I wet the bed. I don't want to wet the bed at my friend's house. At my home, my mom has special sheets on my bed. She doesn't get angry when I have an accident. She says when I get older, I won't wet the bed anymore. When I'm older, I'll go to all the sleepover birthday parties. Now I need to save my face.

We can eat candy and stay up late at sleepovers. One time I slept over and I had an accident. My friend didn't like that the bed was wet. I felt bad when that happened. So, I'll get a little older and then I can sleep over. My mom says one night we can stay up late and eat candy at home. That will be fun, too.

Sounds like you have the best mom. Don't worry about the incident at your friend's. It happens and when you get older, you will get to sleep over more.

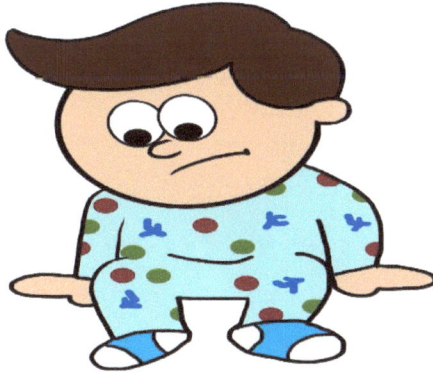

MY STEPFATHER HAS TOO MANY RULES

I'm feeling mad. My stepfather makes too many rules. Now that he lives at our house, we must listen to him. I miss when it was just my mom and me. Last night, I didn't get dessert because I didn't finish my peas. I don't like peas. He doesn't know what foods I like but my mom does. She forgot to tell him.

My stepfather is fun to play with outside. We like to ride bikes. Now I must wear a helmet every time I ride my bike. That strap pinches my chin when he buckles it. I didn't want to wear my helmet, so I got in trouble. I wish there weren't so many rules in my house. My stepfather is not my boss. It makes me angry when he tells me what to do. Mom told me it's right to obey him.

I understand it can be hard, but your stepfather is there to help look out for you. He cares for you, and having rules means that both he and your mom just want the best for you.

MY MOM HAS TO STUDY A LOT

I miss my mom. I like it when she tucks me in, and I love it when she reads me a bedtime story. Not my dad, he doesn't do it very well. My mom must study at night when she gets home from work. My mom wants to be a nurse since she loves to help people. Her school is at nighttime and mine is in the daytime.

Yesterday, my dad had to take me to the bus stop. My mom was already studying that day. She didn't have time to walk me. My dad forgot my gloves, so my hands became very cold. I wish she didn't always have to do homework. When you become a nurse, you must study a lot. My mom is brilliant. I know she will help people because she is gentle, too. But I miss spending time with my mom. I wish to have her back.

Try to be patient. Your dad is doing his best to take care of you. When your mom becomes a nurse, she will have more time.

I HAVE A CAVITY

'm scared. The dentist told my mom I have a cavity. I always brush my teeth, but sometimes, I forget. I usually forget in the morning. My cavity is on my front tooth. My mom says we have to go back to the dentist so she can fix the hole. It will hurt a little. My dentist has a treasure chest, and I can pick out two toys. I want two, little red cars. I hope they have those when I go back.

The dentist told me that my mouth would feel numb for a couple of hours. She said other kids get cavities, too. She gave my mom a new toothbrush. We also have new toothpaste to use. My teeth will be sparkling clean, but I hope it doesn't hurt to get my cavity fixed. I will try to be brave. I must just be.

Yes, you will be brave! They will make your mouth numb so it won't hurt, and it will be over before you know it.

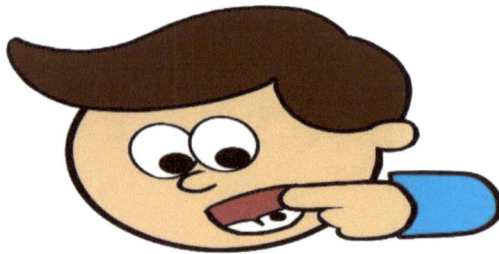

I CAN'T HAVE A TABLET

'm feeling sad. My mom and dad said I couldn't get a tablet. I love to play with my friend's tablet because he can watch movies and play games. My mom says tablets are too much money, and my dad thinks I should play outside. I feel if they played with a tablet, they would like it, also. The car race and temple run are fun.

We could bring it in the car, and then, I wouldn't be so bored when we drive. My dad says I can look out the window but that isn't fun. My friend lets me play with his tablet sometimes, but I really want to get one that's mine. Maybe if I save my allowance, I can get one. Or I might ask Santa. I am sad that I have no tablet just like his.

I know it's frustrating, but you must listen to your mom and dad. Tablets are fun but there are also many other fun things to do, like playing games outdoors with your friends or riding a bike.

MY COUSINS ARE COMING!

I'm feeling very excited! My mom told me my cousins are coming from Colombia! They will stay in my room with my aunt and uncle. Meanwhile, I'll be sleeping in a small bed in my mom's room. I will play with my cousins every day! Mom says that they'll be on the airplane for a long time just like we were. I'm just happy that they'll be staying with us for a long, long time.

I'll show my cousins all my favorite things. The tree on the corner will be their favorite to climb. They'll go to school just like me. I know they will like the swings! When my cousins come, we can walk to school together. I know the way, and I can show them. I want them to come today!

That's very exciting. It sounds like you are going to have a lot of fun with them! I hope I will get to meet them.

THE KIDS LAUGHED AT ME

I'm feeling embarrassed. Today we went to the gym, and there was another class there. We all had to say our name. Then the class would sing our names out loud. When they sang my name, they didn't say it right. The kids all laughed. I didn't like how they sang my name.

The teacher made them do it again. The second time they said it better. But then after class, they said it the mean way again. I don't know why they can't say my name. It's hard for them to say it right. I wish my name was different, and then the kids wouldn't laugh so much. It cracked me up at times, but it is not funny. I always try to say their names the right way. It is not fair.

Your name is unique, and you should be proud of it. Try not to blame them; they laugh because they feel embarrassed that they can't say it right.

MY BROTHER HAS FIGHTS

Teacher, I am scared. Almost every day, my brother has fought. He fights with other boys on our street. We see them when we walk home from school. Every time, my brother says he won't fight. But then he always does! Last week, they ripped his shirt. It was embarrassing!

My mom was mad about the shirt. My brother did not tell her the truth about how it ripped. Why won't my brother tell Mom about the fighting? I'm scared when I see those boys. They always laugh when they see us, but they aren't happy. They're mad and then they fight with my brother. I wish they would stop. I don't want him to get hurt.

Your brother is right that he doesn't need to fight. The next time you see those boys, try and remind your brother of that and just keep walking.

I DON'T LIKE LUNCHTIME

I'm sad. My best friend doesn't sit next to me at lunch anymore. Last week, we sat next to each other. We talked and laughed a lot. The teacher said, "Stop talking and eat!" That made us laugh more, but then another girl made fun of my lunch. She thinks that rice is silly to have for lunch. I have rice every day. So does my best friend. I like it.

Now, my best friend sits with that mean girl. She doesn't eat rice in her lunch anymore. They watch me open my lunch, and then they laugh. It doesn't feel good when they do that. I'm not hungry at lunch anymore. I will eat when I get home instead. I hope my best friend sits with me again. I feel good when she is around me.

Nothing is wrong with eating rice at lunch. It doesn't make sense that they're laughing. Your best friend is not being nice.

I DON'T LIKE RECESS

'm feeling lonely. When I am at school, I don't like to talk. Some kids can't understand me when I talk. They don't know I want to play. I wish I could be their friend, but they can't understand me. In my class last year, I had a friend. He speaks Spanish, but this year, we're in different classes.

I wish he had the same teacher as me so we could play together. We liked to play basketball at recess. Now we don't have recess together. Mom says I should join in when the other kids play. I am too shy to ask them to join in. I hope I make a friend soon. It's boring being alone.

I understand being shy; it is hard. The next time at recess when you want to join a game, try this: give a big smile and ask, "That looks fun. Can I play?"

MY FAMILY WORKS TOO MUCH

'm feeling sad today. All the kids were talking about their vacations. They did fun things with their families. This summer, I went to my neighbor's apartment every day. My family didn't go on any trips. My friends got to ride a roller coaster, but my mom and dad had to work. I didn't go. I like roller coasters, also!

Our neighbor has a little girl. She can walk, but she is a baby. When I brought my toy to their apartment, she broke it. She tore the page of my favorite book. It was from the library! I did not like to play with her. Her toys are for babies. I waited and waited for my mom to get home, but we only had dinner, and then went to bed. I wish we could go on a vacation, too.

Your mom and dad are working hard now so they can provide to take care of you. Have you told your parents you would like to go on vacation?

I DON'T WANT TO RIDE THE BUS

'm feeling worried. The kids on the bus make fun of me. Every day, I have to ride the bus home. That is where the kids laugh at me. They say I smell and my clothes look strange. They don't say it aloud; they say it quietly. I can hear them when they make fun of me. I walk to the back of the bus as fast as I can.

One boy follows me all the time. He changes his seat and sits next to the seat I pick in the back. Then, he says mean things to me. I wish he would stay in the front. I don't like it when he does that. The bus driver can't hear him. The boy used to make fun of another kid, but now he makes fun of me. I wish he would pick another kid. I wish he would leave me alone or get caught.

That boy does not sound like a nice person! Next time, try sitting as close to the front of the bus you can, so if the boy picks on you again, the bus driver may hear.

MY BIRTHDAY IS COMING!

I'm so happy! This weekend, it's my birthday! My family will have a big party for me. All my cousins will be coming to see me. My aunts and uncles will come, too! My mom and my grandmother and my aunts will cook all my favorite foods. My friends in my building will come! We will play music and dance!

Everyone loves parties in my family. I love to dance with my mom. My little brother dances too, but he is just a baby, so he falls, and everyone laughs. My uncle is the best dancer of all! We have so much fun at parties! I hope my mom and grandmother hang balloons and streamers for me in the backyard. And then everyone will sing 'Happy Birthday' to me! I can't wait for my birthday party!

That is very exciting! Happy Birthday – how old will you be this weekend?

MY GOLDFISH DIED

'm feeling sad because my goldfish just died. When I came home from school, he wasn't swimming anymore. My mom and I drew a picture of him so I can remember him always. He had a pretty tail: it was red, orange, and a little bit of yellow. He liked to hide behind the castle in his tank. Mom said he liked the bubbles there from the filter.

I'll miss seeing him when I come home from school. Every day, I knew that I could see him and look at his beautiful tail. My sisters weren't allowed to touch his tank because I considered him to be just mine. I cleaned his tank once a month and fed him every day. Now we have leftover food. The tank is empty, and I feel sad when I look at it. Mom says we can get another fish soon, but I wish I had my goldfish back. I have got used to him.

I'm sorry that your goldfish died, that is sad! Did you hang the picture of him on your wall so you can always see it?

MY BROTHER GETS ALL THE ATTENTION

My brother is older than me. He is good at school, he gets good grades, and he helps my dad at the store after school. Mom says I'm too young to help at the store. My brother is allowed to ride his bike to school. I have to take the bus with the neighbors next door. My brother has a lot of friends. I see him playing at school with his friends every day. They don't let me play with them.

At home, I always get in trouble when we fight. My mom says I should leave my brother alone. He needs to do his homework. I wish he would play with me or we could do our homework together. My brother gets to use my dad's desk and I don't. My mom makes all his favorite foods at dinner. My brother gets to talk more at dinner, too. Then he gets to stay up later! I wish I could do the same things as my brother. I feel jealous of him. I can't wait to grow up.

Try not to fight with your brother. You will grow up soon. You are just as smart as he is, and if you work hard, you will get good grades, too!

ABOUT THE AUTHOR

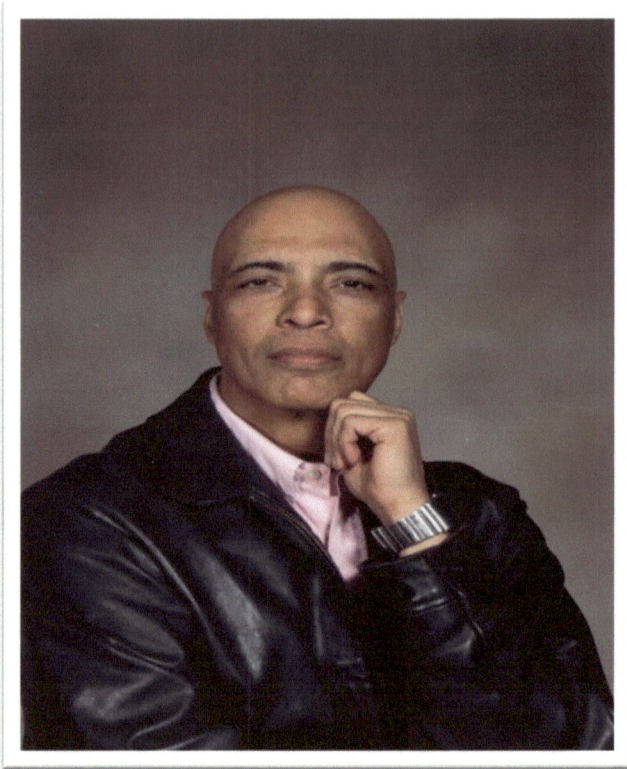

Sabat Beatto is a popular author with over twenty books for children and adults in a variety of genres.

BOOKS BY SABAT BEATTO

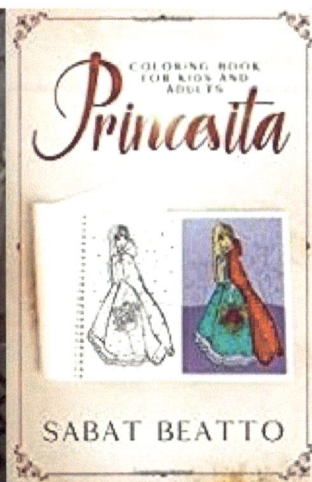

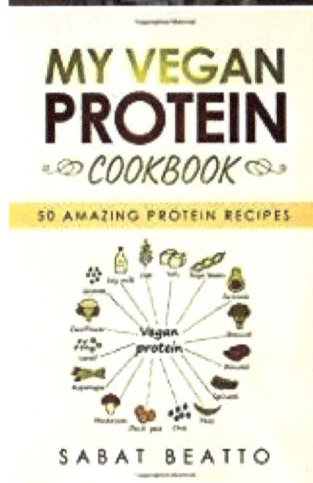

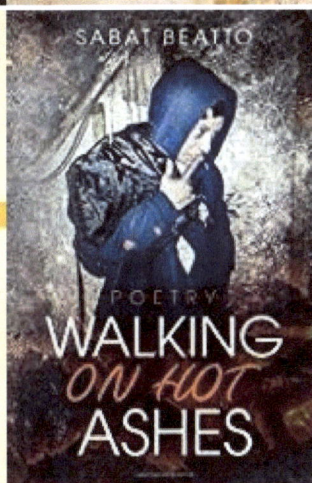

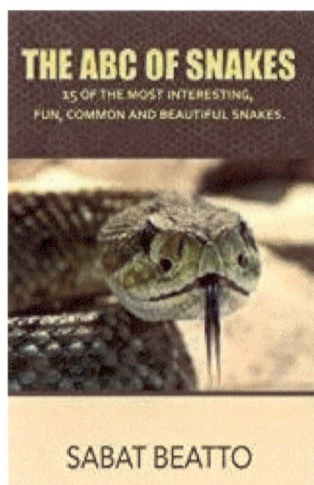

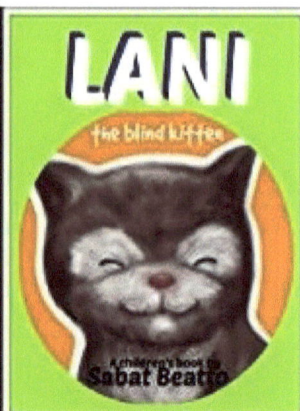

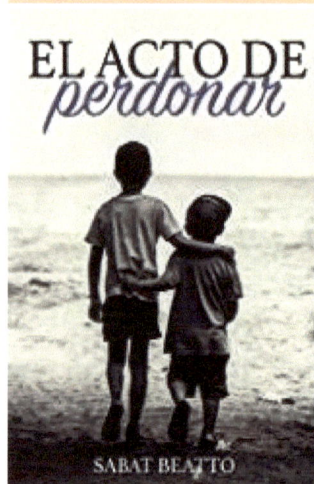

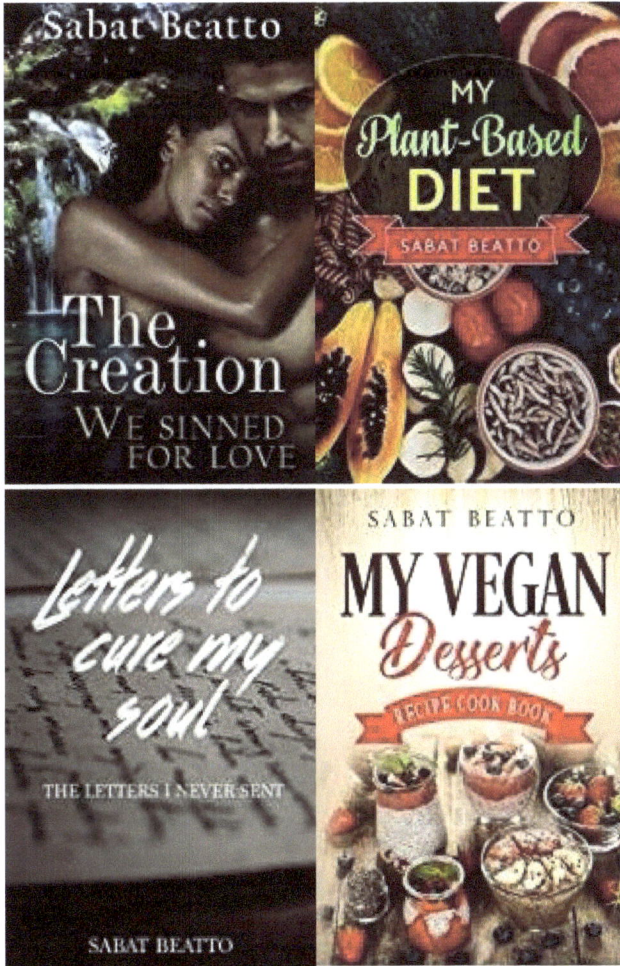

www.ingramcontent.com/pod-product-compliance
Lightning Source LLC
Chambersburg PA
CBHW041806040426
42448CB00005B/292